"Possibly the greatest book ever written. Ever."
Amanda's mum

"If you've ever thought that crafting clever words for your business was a dark, unmasterable art, this book is for you. Amanda breaks down how to Write Better, into small deliciously enjoyable chunks of goodness. With easy to understand advice, practical tips and relatable examples, this book should be on the desk of every business owner."
Kate Toon – Author | Speaker | Copywriter | SEO expert

"Practical, fun and full of writing tips that shouldn't be secrets. Buy this book, borrow this book or steal it off your friend's desk."
Peter Crocker – Writer | Editor

"Oh Amanda… a kindred spirit! You totally validated my love of white space, dot points and red pens. This is THE book for all grammar and language nerds and for the Maries (see intro!) of the world…you'll never embarrass yourself again. Should be on the desk of anyone required to string a few words together. It's full of aha moments delivered with a fabulous sense of humour. A clever, informative and well crafted guide to how to Write Better. Highly recommended!"
Sandra D – Grammar enthusiast | Language nerd

"Loved it! So very easy to read. Such great, practical advice and easy to understand examples. Lots of great information for newbies just starting out, and some absolute gems for old-timers who think they know it all. It would be a great present for all university graduates to undo everything they've been taught and make them ready for writing in the real world."

Estelle Fallon - Copywriter

"We are all writers, whether we like it or not. Every email we send and social media post we create is testament to this. Amanda's book takes writing advice out of the realm of grammar geeks and makes real-life writing easier for real-life people. Everyone should have a copy on their desks for those moments where the blinking cursor paralyses them into inaction."

Kelly Exeter - Author | Editor | Ghostwriter

"Do as she says. It's easier that way."

Amanda's husband

"Amanda's book is full of sound advice for those who struggle to write, as well as for the seasoned pro. How you write is key to communicating clearly and having your ideas understood. Don't just write well - Write Better!"

Andrew C Lau - Writer

"Mandatory reading for every high school and university student and first year grad... actually mandatory for anyone that has to write...anything. Amanda breaks down those complex grammar theories from yesteryear into easy tips and tricks on how to write better. Including a ransom note. And for the record... I agree 'red pen' should always be a verb and emojis are life."

Anna Vinfield - Communications Specialist and Smarty Pants

"As a writer and teacher of writers, I've read hundreds (not kidding) of writing books. This one is the most straightforward, practical, and helpful handbook on writing in today's world. It gave me goosebumps. It made me laugh. It made me want to hunt down all the people in my past life who wanted me to put more stupid words into my content and scream, 'See! THIS is why I write plain English!' and beat them over the head with it.

Amanda cuts through all the crap that is part of so much writing at work and in life, and shows you how to write clear, direct, and purposeful messages. She gives you the questions to ask, the structure to use, examples to follow, and the best tips on how to write a ransom note that I've ever seen.

This book can help us all write better."

Rochelle Bright - Poet | Writing Teacher

"Thank goodness you stuck with the word stuff."

All of Amanda's math teachers

write better

HOW TO CUT THE CRAP AND SAY WHAT YOU MEAN

Copyright © 2018 by Amanda Vanelderen
All rights reserved.

Published in Australia by Write Better
www.writebetter.com.au

National Library of Australia Publication Data
available via www.nla.gov.au

ISBN: 978-0-6483027-0-4

Printed in Australia

Cover and Interior Design:
Swish Design | swishdesign.com.au

Illustrations:
ALW Clarke | alwclarke.com

First Edition

For my family

contents

Introduction 1
    Life's too short for crap writing 2
    How did we get here? 2
    Why you need to write better 3
    Who is this guide for? 3
    So you think you're not a writer 4
    Real writing advice for real people 5
    How to use this guide 6
The Write Better Manifesto 7
Before you write 9
    It's all about APPLES 11
    Understand your AUDIENCE 12
    Be clear on your PURPOSE 14
    PLAN how you'll get your message across 16
    Use the right LANGUAGE 20
    Be prepared to EDIT 29

Plan out your STRUCTURE 31

So, how about them APPLES? 35

Your super simple guide to getting started. 37

Your super simple guide to Plain English 43

Your super simple guide to writing faster. 51

Your super simple guide to grammar and punctuation 57

Your super simple guide to editing and proofreading 65

Your super simple guide to emojis 77

The CRAP FILES 83

Write better emails 87

Write better job stuff. 95

Write better ransom notes. 105

Write better presentations. 113

Write better apologies. 121

Write better headlines and headings 129

Write better blogs 135

Write better social media 141

Time to wrap up 149

What next?. 153

Acknowledgements 155

write better

HOW TO CUT THE CRAP AND SAY WHAT YOU MEAN

AMANDA VANELDEREN

introduction

I was 23, and my boss[1] was a bully.

She hated me because the head honchos praised my writing. Worse still, she made me second guess what I could do.

So when the opportunity came to write a high-profile recruitment campaign, she took it on herself. She wrote it, and didn't bother to get it proofread.

She smelled glory.

That weekend her half-page ad ran in every national newspaper, asking for applicants with 'extensive experience in pubic relations'.

Yep.

Pubic relations.

Liberated, I left soon after.

---

[1] Let's call her Marie. Everyone else does.

Life's too short for crap writing

It takes longer to write, and longer to read. It can also be embarrassing (see previous page).

If you ever feel lost, agonise over emails, or live in fear of others judging your work, I've got good news for you.

Everyone has it in them to write better.

But first ...

How did we get here?

Pressure to meet word counts means we're using more filler than a Kardashian. And when brands shout at us, they're teaching us to ignore nuance and meaning.

Our heads are up our bums about punctuation and old-school writing rules, so we spend our time shaming typos instead of judging whether something makes sense.

Luckily there are ways you can cut the crap, find the right words for your audience, and build your writing confidence.

Why you need to write better

We're taking in 78 kazillion[2] messages every day.

Clear communication is a big advantage in the great game of life. It helps you develop ideas, make logical arguments, and build a reputation as someone people want on their team.

You'll also save time, stand out and feel good.

Who is this guide for?

Everyone who loves words, and anyone who doesn't.

People who love writing (or want to).

Everyday people who don't think they're writers but write every day (see the next page).

Word nerds, grammar geeks and lexicon lovers.

And anyone whose boss told them to write better if they want to get a pay rise.

---

[2] Made-up stat.

So you think you're *not* a writer

But I bet you ...

Spend your days sending emails.

Post on social media.

Deliver presentations.

Send out email newsletters.

Jot down ransom notes.

Respond to complaints and compliments.

Apply for grants or tenders.

Publish reports and meeting minutes.

Develop policies and procedures.

Draft ads for the local paper.

Update a staff intranet.

The truth is, **we're ALL writers**, whether we like it or not. But, I get it. You're sick of reading writing advice for writerly types. That's why I wrote this book. I wanted to offer ...

Real writing advice for real people

This book steps you through:

- putting your audience in the spotlight
- nailing your structure
- using language that works.

I'll help you **banish your fear of the blank page** by sharing tips on getting started, drafting, editing and proofreading.

I'll give you rules, guidelines, tips, tricks and secret passwords. And then show you when to ignore them all.

You'll also learn the **small changes that can make a big difference**.

By the end of the book you'll have put it all into practice: writing emails, ransom notes, presentations, job stuff, social media updates – the lot!

How to use this guide

Scribble on it[3], stick Post-It notes on it, and highlight it to death. Skip the parts that bore you, and re-read the parts you love. Keep it on your desk at work, your home office, the glovebox or your go bag[4]. Love it hard, however you want.

Ready to go? Let's get to it!

Amanda

Warning: cutting the crap is addictive. Soon you'll want to red pen[5] newspapers, flyers, online ads, signs and emails from your mum. Don't say I didn't warn you!

---

[3] Not the library copy, you animal. | [4] A bag shady types have packed and ready to 'go' at a moment's notice. May contain fake passports, international currencies and peroxide. | [5] It's a verb here.

the write better manifesto

These are the rules and philosophies I live by when I write. Everything I'm going to share in this book comes back to these 10 things, so feel free to use this manifesto as an 'anchor' for all your writing efforts.

1. Write for your audience
2. Get to the point, then get out
3. Write to be scanned *and* for the person who reads every word
4. Plan your writing to be understood the first time
5. Big words don't make you look smart
6. Write to make someone's day
7. Truth is always the easiest explanation
8. Credibility is crucial (and likeability doesn't hurt either)
9. Use formatting, structure and images to support your words
10. Alway, ALWAYS respect your audience and their time

BEFORE YOU write

It's all about APPLES

Writing better starts before you type a single word.

You need to:

- Understand your **AUDIENCE**.
- Be clear on your **PURPOSE**.
- **PLAN** how you'll get your message across.
- Write in the tone of voice and **LANGUAGE** to suit your audience.
- Go in prepared to **EDIT** and rewrite to get it right.
- Plan a **STRUCTURE** so the right words are in the right place.

Let's take a closer look at each of these ...

Understand your AUDIENCE

The best way to develop an understanding of your audience is to **get to know them**. How can you do this?

1. Ask them questions

Talk to them. Interview them. Use surveys, testimonials and reviews to find out what they like (and don't like) and **what they want** from you.

2. Access data

Real stats from credible sources give you some powerful insights into the problems they want solved.

3. Hang out

Find out where your audience gathers online—Facebook groups, Instagram, Twitter, Pinterest, Snapchat, Reddit, industry forums or wherever—and go hang out in those places too.

It's a chance to learn the language they use, find out what's important to them, and **crack their code**.

SHOW ME

What's the difference between a piece of writing that knows its audience and one that doesn't? Let's look at a short introduction inviting parents to a school open day.

NO audience research (all you know about your audience is that they're parents with school-aged kids)

   Come to the Mooville Independent School.

SOME audience research (you found out traffic is a huge local issue)

   When your children are part of the Mooville Independent School community, they'll get home sooner.

MORE audience research (you learned about the traffic issue, how the average income has risen in the past two years, and that parents in local FB groups are concerned about teenage safety and behaviour)

   *You can't put a price on your child's safety. Get them home sooner by making them part of the Mooville Independent School community.*

🍎 Be clear on your PURPOSE

If you don't know the purpose behind what you're writing, you need to step away from the keyboard and ask yourself some questions.

1. What's the 'why'?

Another way to put this is, '**What's the outcome you want** from this piece of writing?' Are you trying to:

- Persuade?
- Sell a thing or an idea?
- Ask for help?
- Apologise?
- Explain?
- Give good or bad news?
- Solve a problem?

2. What's the big idea?

Everything you write should have **one big idea** you're trying to communicate. (Yes, even an email.)

When you know the basic 'why' of your piece, and you link it to your big idea, **your purpose becomes crystal clear.**

SHOW ME

How can you tell a piece of writing that knows it's why and big idea from one that doesn't? Let's look at a flyer asking you to complete a survey about your neighbourhood.

 A FLYER WITH NO WHY OR BIG IDEA

Neighbourhood survey

Please see link below to online survey about our neighbourhood.

Thank you
Mr. Incognito

 A FLYER WITH A WHY AND A BIG IDEA

Why: Gather information to decide how to use funding
Big idea: Better facilities in our suburb build a sense of community

Help build a community to be proud of

We're pleased to announce the Neighbourhood Association has received a community grant to invest in new facilities.

Please speak up and tell us what you think. Where can the money make a difference to build a safe and healthy community where everyone can live their best lives?

Your voice counts. Have your say in the survey at neighbourprojectsurvey.com

 PLAN how you'll get your message across

Once you're clear on the 'why' behind your piece and the big idea you're trying to communicate, it's time to **make a plan**.

Why? Because you write faster when you have a plan. Here's a simple, three-step outline for any piece of writing.

1. Hook their interest

Complement your big idea with something to sweeten the deal, keep their attention, and **make it worth their time** to read.

Outright bribery works as a hook:

> *'Here's a 10% discount.'*

Immediacy works too:

> *'No six-week training course required, you'll see results right away.'*

2. Make them feel something

Whatever the big idea is, you want your audience to **feel something** so you can make a connection and take them on a journey.

Put on your audience hat and dig deeper into the basic emotions humans want to feel:

- like they're understood
- like they belong
- hopeful and inspired
- strong and confident
- like they have something to believe in.

Decide how you want them to feel, then **follow it up with what you need** from the interaction.

3. Tell them what to do

It might be to buy something from you, respond to your email, or agree to your idea.

Provide a clear call to action and **make it easy for them** to do that thing whether it's to reply, click the link or make the booking. Don't put the brakes on. Let them floor it.

SHOW ME

Let's put it into practice and **map out a simple plan**. You're writing an email to a new customer of your pet supplies business about a members-only community for Chihuahua owners, ChiChi Boots.

What's the big idea we're trying to communicate?

We love Chihuahuas.

What's the 'why' behind this email?

Persuade them to join the members-only community.

How will we hook their interest?

25% discount code on signup.

What will make them feel something?

Belong to a secret club with products and discounts = exclusivity.

We care about our pets as much as they do = kinship.

What do we want them to do?

Click for instant signup (direct them to the online shop with discount code automatically applied).

This simple plan means you have something to work with before putting pen to paper. Now, let's see what the email might look like.

Keep your Chi warm this winter with 25% off legwarmers for your precious pup

Winter is coming... and that means shivers for our Chihuahuas!

Join the ChiChi Boots family today for an instant 25% discount on supplies for the Chi in your life.

Full of Chi care advice, giveaways, dress up competitions and ChiChi fun, our updates bring the world's most adorable doggies to your inbox every month.

We love our Chis as much as you do. From Chihuahua legwarmers to the latest in luxury bedding, we've got you and your fur baby covered ... from head to toe!

Join the ChiChi family today.

🍎 Use the right LANGUAGE

Choosing the right language and tone for your audience ensures you're able to connect with them, and **get them to listen to you**!

Here are some tips for ensuring you're hitting the mark.

1. Be crystal clear

Your end game is to be understood. Don't hide your message under waffle words, clunky sentences and funky phrases.

Remember, **you're writing for humans** so it's okay to sound like one.

2. Stop clearing your throat

Sentences often start with loads of waffling and unnecessary words. **There's no need to clear your throat** (like a giant "Ahem") before you get to the point. Don't ask for permission to give an opinion, or use extra words as padding to reach a magical word count. Every wasted word gives your reader another reason to scroll (or stroll) away.

SHOW ME

Here's how to start weeding out some of the worst throat-clearing offenders. (I've also made some sneaky edits to tighten the language up.)

 So to get going, we started by scheduling a meeting.

 We scheduled a meeting.

 Needless to say, the event started on time.

 The event started on time.

 In the interests of time, we'll try to keep this meeting brief.

 We'll keep this meeting brief.

 It is apparent that bees are attracted to flowers.

 Bees are attracted to flowers.

3. Step away from the thesaurus

Big words don't make you look smart. They make you look like you've got something to hide. **If you wouldn't say it, odds are you shouldn't write it.**

Using unfamiliar words tells your readers you aren't interested in them, or that you're going to make them feel stupid. You don't always have to be super casual. Just use everyday words.

4. Ditch the adverbs

Remember adverbs? (They're qualifying words that change or emphasise meaning of the word next to them.) Now forget them. Writing becomes stronger when you **delete words like:**

- actually
- completely
- greatly
- suddenly
- seriously.
- basically
- currently
- presently
- very

SHOW ME

Here's how your writing becomes better when you take adverbs out of the action. The third example shows how your statement becomes even stronger if you remove the qualifiers of 'I believe' and 'can'.

 I truly believe we can transform our business greatly by completely updating our website.

 I believe we can transform our business by updating our website.

 *Updating our website will transform our business.*

TIP

Take the advice of Mark Twain. Use the word 'damn' every time you want to write 'very'. Then let your editor delete them all.

5. Don't be tone deaf

Tone of voice is the **attitude you bring to your writing**. It sets the mood for the reader. You have unlimited choices in the tone you use, so choose one that suits *both* your audience and your big idea.

For example, you may want to sound:

- approachable and generous
- formal and professional
- elegant and exclusive
- smart and innovative
- warm and friendly
- casual and funny.

Thinking about the tone before you write helps you **plan how to get your message across** and choose words to back it up.

But whatever tone you choose, try to be likeable. And resist the urge to get too clever or make everything you write sound the same. Sometimes the best gift you can give your reader is to be straightforward.

> ## No smoking
>
> *Consistency is key to making your tone work. I was reading a high-end jewellery site with an **elegant and exclusive** tone. In an article on the history of wedding rings, they mentioned that rings were originally made from hemp, then worked in a joke about smoking the rings to relieve wedding stress. It was a **massive clanger**, and the spell was broken.*

6. Trade in hesitating words

We **are committed to** providing the highest levels of customer support...

We **aim to** deliver...

We **try to** provide the...

Can, could, might, will, should...

Ugh.

Hesitation and caveats in your writing imply you're hedging your bets and introduces doubt. **Be definite, be confident**, and don't take a backwards step.

SHOW ME

DELETE: Get rid of those hesitating words when you can confidently stand behind what you're saying.

 Fridgetopia can make sure you get the best fridge possible that meets your needs.

 At Fridgetopia, get the fridge to meet your needs.

 *Your fridge dreams come true at Fridgetopia.*

KEEP: Less definite or indirect language is fine when you're constrained by what you can say.

 AwesomeApples Vitamins cure disease.

 AwesomeApples Vitamins may help cure some diseases.

 *Boost your health and wellbeing with AwesomeApples Vitamins.*

7. Take the focus off you

Starting sentences with 'I', 'We' or 'Our' is **a bad language habit** that takes the focus off your audience. And we know there is nothing more important than our audience, don't we? Fortunately, it's a habit that's easy to spot and to break.

SHOW ME

Here's how to shift the focus away from you and shine the spotlight firmly on your customer.

 Our team is experienced in finding new fridges to add to our extensive range.

 You'll find the biggest range of fridges to choose from at Fridgetopia.

 *Your dream fridge is waiting at Fridgetopia.*

In defence of jargon

Most writing guides will tell you point blank not to use jargon.

But this isn't most writing guides.

Spoiler alert: in most cases you shouldn't use jargon. But one person's jargon is another's **shortcut to shared understanding**. *Filler, waffle words and padding are the real enemies.*

If jargon, specific terms and slang work for your audience, use them. The right jargon can become your **secret writing weapon.**

🍎 Be prepared to EDIT

Ruthless editing makes your writing better.

If you write perfectly first time, every time, I salute you (and laugh at your lies). As someone smart once said, writing is rewriting. And editing. And maybe more rewriting.

By thinking about editing and rewriting before you write, you can **plan a process** that gives you permission not to get it right the first time.

(This is the entree to the why of editing. See page 65 for the main course of how.)

Make the time

You've got a long to-do list, not enough time, and deadlines coming out your ears. But here's the rub: **knowing you get to edit means you can write the first draft faster**. And if writing gets you what you want, do you have time not to do it?

Respect your audience

If you're in charge of the schedule, get the content **moving as early as possible** so there's enough time for a thorough editing process. Leaving the writing until the last minute so there's no time for edits or tweaks isn't respecting your audience.

Trust the butterflies

*Writing for a living, **I still get butterflies when someone edits my work**. I feel lost about where to start and what to say, and always wish I had more time to make it better.*

*It's easy to forget when people praise your writing. **But it's hard to shake feedback that cuts you to the quick**, like the lawyer who described my first draft as "undecipherable", and the real estate client who told me, "you're just not getting it".*

*But **feedback (and wanting to nail what others need from you) makes you a better writer**. Trust me.*

🍎 Plan out your STRUCTURE

A **logical flow of ideas** makes your writing easy to understand, compelling and engaging. The right structure creates a framework to colour in (and cover in glitter).

Go with the flow

Every sentence and paragraph needs to have a point. Each should lead neatly into the next in a logical order.

Take your audience on a smooth and comfortable ride and they'll read on without having to make a conscious decision. Get the structure wrong, and you'll interrupt your reader and jolt them out of the moment.

> **TIP**
>
> **Remember, you don't need to get the flow perfect on your first go.** Sometimes what I write in my first draft shakes up my plan and I see a better structure or focus for what I'm writing.

The beauty of 3 and other odd numbers

The rule of three is as old as time, and taps into how the human brain works. Having three things in a list or story provokes comparison, allows the brain to recognise a pattern, and is **easier to remember**.

Odd numbers also have more weight when you write. As a general rule, being **specific looks more authentic, accurate and interesting.** Do you want to read about 60 ways to write better, or 67? The odd number implies you've written as much as you know, whereas 60 implies you had a target.

See how the rule of three and specific odd numbers create more engaging, readable and authentic wording.

RULE OF THREE

 Simple and practical

 Simple, practical, and ready to use

SPECIFIC ODD NUMBERS

 How I got 5000 Instagram followers

 How I got 4,987 Instagram followers

Be a mix master

Smart writing doesn't mean making everything sound the same. We don't use the same number of words in every sentence we speak, so why do it when we write? Mix it up and get a rhythm going.

It's okay to **use an unexpected sentence length**, or even a one-line paragraph.

It keeps everyone guessing.

Phone it in

Knowing your audience also means knowing how and where they read what you write. We live in a digital world, **so smartphones and mobile devices must be part of your plan for structuring your writing.**

Think about how you read on your screen. You scan headings, look at images, and then (maybe) go back for a closer look.

Writing for the phone screen means saying less, getting to the point quickly, and **not giving your reader thumbache** *by making them scroll to find what they need.*

Formatting stuff

Formatting won't save poor writing. But it can **put the important stuff in the spotlight.**

Hot tips for cool structure:

- Use dot points if it suits your audience.
- Use meaningful **headings and subheadings** in a consistent style.
- Use pictures, drawings and infographics to complement what you write. (And make their labels interesting too.)
- Reference any figures, tables or graphs within the text. If you don't, why is it there?
- Use pull quotes or highlight boxes to **give your reader a break**.
- **De-chunkify**[6] big paragraphs and sentences into bite-sized pieces. Don't hide **golden nuggets of information** away in fat paragraphs no one will read.

---

[6] Not a real word. Yet.

So, how about them APPLES?

Let's recap! You now know you can speed up your writing process by first taking the time before you write to:

- Understand your **AUDIENCE**.
- Be clear on your **PURPOSE**.
- **PLAN** how you'll get your message across.
- Understand the tone of voice and **LANGUAGE** that best suits your audience.
- Get prepared to **EDIT** and rewrite to get it right.
- Plan a **STRUCTURE** so the right words are in the right place.

What's next? It's time to put pen to paper...

YOUR Super Simple GUIDE TO GETTING STARTED

Einstein was a smart guy. He knew success was 1% talent and 99% sweat. He didn't sit back and wait for inspiration to strike. He showed up and did the work.

Be like Einstein.

The blank page isn't the enemy once you realise you can fill it however you want. Here are seven ways to **trick yourself into getting started** when that blinking cursor is driving you crazy.

1. Start with the headings

When I'm stuck, I start by writing the headline and subheadings for my article, email or whatever. It helps me structure what I'm going to write and **get some ideas flowing**.

Once you've done that, go back and throw dot points under each one, or add questions or things to look up. Now **the page is dirty**, and you're on your way.

2. Fill the page with crap

Don't try to form the perfect words in your head. **Writing is part of the thinking process** and it allows ideas to clarify. It helps you make sense of your work and what you need to say. Do you think I wrote this book in the time it took me to type these words? Yeah, nah.

3. Go 'old school'

Go 'old school' and brainstorm with a pen and paper. Write down your big idea, and draw squiggly lines and flow charts[7]. Just the act of scribbling can engage your brain in another way and **spark something**. And it's fun.

---

[7] And maybe a little house.

4. Start at the end

Write down your conclusion—where you want the article to end. **Working backwards helps** you learn what your audience needs to know.

5. Use Post-It notes

Take a Post-It note and write down everything you know about your topic. Make dot points and fill that sucker up—both sides. Now type up what you've written. **Your muscle memory will kick in and you'll keep going.** Trust me.

6. Trick yourself

Commit to writing for 10-15 minutes without any distractions. Set a timer, and promise yourself you can walk away when it goes off. Worst-case scenario, you've done 10-15 minutes of writing you wouldn't have done otherwise. But there's a good chance you'll **find a thread and keep going.**

7. Create a deadline

Deadlines are the cruellest and kindest of creatures.

If you're a master of creative excuses, look for some **outside accountability**. Arrange to check in with a colleague or friend (the 'tough love' kind), or let your audience know they'll be reading your thing on Thursday. **It'll get the fires burning.**

YOUR Super Simple GUIDE TO PLAIN ENGLISH

Plain English (or plain language) is a way of writing and speaking using **simple, everyday language**. It doesn't mean stripping away your individual voice, creativity or sense of fun.

Plain English inspires action. By providing clear information and next steps, **you speak directly to your audience, connect with them and move them forward**. It's the easiest way to get your point across and get your reader to do something—not a way to dumb it down.

Why use Plain English?

It puts your reader at the centre of what you're doing, just as they should be. It's faster to write, faster to read, and more likely to be understood.

Huh?

*I saw a politician discussing a new policy. He referred to making a **Plain English version** available. Why do we need both? Shouldn't the Plain English version be the one we all read?*

TIPS

Plain English is not the same as Easy English.
Easy English is a way of writing for people who have difficulty reading and understanding English. It uses simple wording, minimal punctuation and images to communicate key points without too much detail.

Reading and understanding aren't the same thing.
Even people you know who communicate well mightn't have the written literacy levels you'd expect. Plain English is a tool to make sure people with literacy issues, or people from culturally and linguistically diverse (CALD) backgrounds all have the **same access to information and knowledge** as anyone else. It's their right.

Writing to be understood

The choices you make in language, structure, and sentences all play a part in getting your message across in a simple way.

1. Use everyday words

- Choose words your audience would use and understand
- **Explain jargon** and technical terms
- Avoid overusing words like 'that', 'which' and 'and'

2. Formatting and style

- Use dot points and make lists
- Add **meaningful headings** and subheadings
- Explain how images, graphs and tables relate to your message

3. Get active

- Use **active language**—'you' and 'we' instead of 'the applicant' or 'the customer'[8]
- Focus on sounding professional, not bureaucratic
- Use an active voice so it's clear who is doing what[9] (but keep an eye on when passive voice works for your reader)

---

[8] Call these personal pronouns if you want to get fancy.
[9] It nauseates me to discuss subject, action and agent.
If you want to know more, Google is waiting.

SHOW ME

WHEN TO BE ACTIVE ...

 *The man **was bitten by** the lonely giraffe.*

 *The lonely giraffe **bit** the man.*

 ***It is believed** by the investigators that the giraffe **must be placed** in custody by the police.*

 ***The investigators believe** the police **must place** the giraffe in custody.*

WHEN TO BE PASSIVE ...

Use passive voice if you need to take the sting out of a message or make it less personal. Use:

- **The processes were overlooked** instead of **Joe overlooked the processes.**
- **The bill hasn't been paid** instead of **You haven't paid the bill.**

4. Short and sweet

- Use short words
- Use short sentences. And longer sentences. **Mix up the pace** so it stays interesting and readable
- Use short paragraphs with a clear point

5. Language

- Use verbs, not nouns. 'Decided' instead of 'made a decision', and 'contributed' instead of 'make a contribution'
- **Break phrases down** to fewer words without losing meaning. Say 'daily' instead of 'on a daily basis'

TIP

If you use 'and' more than once in your sentence, it's probably too long. If you need to take more than one breath when you read it aloud, it's definitely too long.

SHOW ME

Here's a paragraph you may find in a government or corporate response. A Plain English approach takes it from unreadable to simple.

In relation to the feedback you have outlined in your letter regarding the application form and process available on our website, I would like to advise you that our application processes are continuously reviewed on an ongoing basis to ensure that they are as user-friendly as possible and consequently that they are as accessible as possible to everyone. I will ensure that your valuable feedback is considered as we undertake to consider a review of our application processes at a future time[10].

Thank you for your feedback about our application process. We'll consider your suggestions when we review the process.

If you have any questions, please call 1300 WRITE BETTER.

---

[10] I'm going to guess most people don't read this at all. Point proven.

Writing faster doesn't mean getting it over with quickly. It means seeing the first draft as one part of the process. **Writing fast means you can let something sit, have time to edit**, and rewrite it if you need to.

Done, not perfect, should be the goal

Aim to get your first draft **done, not perfect**. Let the sentences be clunky and your paragraphs vague. You have permission to get that paper dirty and empty all the ideas floating in your brain onto the page.

Find accountability

Don't have a set deadline for something? Set one. **Tell someone your writing goal**—a friend, a workmate, your next-door neighbour's cousin's dog walker. (Apparently this is how you can get a book written too.) Tell people it's happening and then you've got to do it.

Limit your research time

Resist going down the online rabbit hole and looking for more information. At some point, you have to start writing. If you have gaps in your research, make a note and **look stuff up later**.

Read all about it

One of my first 'proper' writing jobs was **summarising news articles** *for a media clips company. Starting at 2am, we'd take our bundle of newspaper clippings (yes, newspapers used to be made of paper, kids) and write 50-word summaries of each article. It was an awesome* **training ground for fast writing**. *(Not to mention saving constantly. The computer system would regularly crash. Ctrl-S is now like a tic for me as I write.)*

Trust the process

Write fast and don't worry about spelling, whether your commas are in the right spots, or whether over-thinking should be hyphenated. Leave that for editing.

Set a word limit

Throw minimum word counts on their head and limit yourself to keeping it brief. It's amazing how **short and sweet** you can be when you've set a limit of 150 characters or less for your intro sentence or 40 characters for your email subject line[11].

---

[11] Personal favourite for this word limit geek.

Chase down your ideas with a pen (or a keyboard)

You don't need to know exactly what you want to say before you start to write. The act of writing—typing or handwriting—helps get you there.

Millions of thoughts drift lazily through our noggins every day. Others shoot through at such speed we'll never know they existed. But the sneakiest of all walk just ahead of us so we never quite catch up. Writing helps us think, develop ideas, and **grab those pesky thoughts by the ankles**.

Keep a swipe file

Get a kickstart to faster writing by looking at how someone else did it. When you see a turn of phrase, or a way of presenting information or a catchy heading you like, **file it all away (literally or in your brain bank).**

I flick through all my junk mail before I toss it in the recycling bin. The worst of it makes me despair, the best of it makes me want to write better. And all of it reminds me why words are so important.

YOUR Super Simple GUIDE TO (grammar and punctuation)

Grammar and punctuation aren't crap. But the way we're taught them *is*. And **language rules and conventions are always changing**. It's evolution, baby.

Without some grammar and punctuation basics no-one will read what you write, your ideas will get lost, and you'll be judged as both a writer and human being. Harsh, but true.

The good news is **the basics are easy to remember and use**.

Consistency is everything

Whatever writing quirks or mistakes creep in, **you can get away with them** if you're consistent. Yes, your cred slips if your grammar or punctuation is off. But consistency is more important.

If you choose to hyphenate a word and you're not sure if it's technically correct, **double down and hyphenate** every one of those suckers.

Basic stuff you need to know

◉ Full stops

Put a full stop at the end of a sentence. Be consistent on whether or not you put one at the end of dot points. Don't put one at the end of headings. Pretty please.

❝ Speech marks

Ah, the curse of every online news article. If you're quoting someone, add a comma after what they say (before the speech marks) if they're going to continue on. If they've finished, add a full stop before the speech mark.

Mr Jones said, "Tell me a fairytale."

"And if you won't," he said, "I'll cry myself to sleep."

> **TIP**
>
> **Inappropriate use of apostrophes** is the punctuation 'crime' most likely to irritate the grammar pedants around you. My take on apostrophes? Try to use them properly, but don't lose sleep over them.

🔵 Apostrophes

These can show ownership or a relationship to someone or something, or where letters are missing if two words are combined.

Lucia and Liam's wedding wasn't ruined by yesterday's storm.

When it comes to last names, default to adding an 's' with no apostrophe.

Merry Christmas from the Vanelderens.

🔵 Colons

Use it to start a list. Most of the time, it's better to present lists as dot points than a chunk of text.

🔵 Commas

Put a comma where you'd take a breath if you were reading aloud, or if it helps your reader make sense of a sentence. Too many commas means the sentence is too long.

🔵 Exclamation marks

Try to limit yourself to one per page or block of writing.

● hyphens ● en dashes ● em dashes

Hyphens connect related things e.g. over-punctuation, two-thirds.

En dashes connect spans and imply the inclusion of what's in the middle e.g. pages 101–107.

Em dashes let you add an aside or an endnote to a sentence—something related that could be taken out and the sentence would still make sense—and also to imply something has been removed. They can also be used as a kind of bullet point.

; Semicolon

Odds are you won't use a semicolon correctly. It's not your fault. Forget them in the name of sanity and reader experience. Sometimes you'll need them at the end of list items, but if you give them a wide berth as a rule, no-one will miss them.

> **TIP**
>
> **Even professional writers rewrite sentences to avoid a clumsy plural or punctuation conundrum.** I will never write '10 years' experience' when I could write '10 years of experience'. And while full stops are important, I'll change my sentence to avoid ending on an email or web address when I'm not sure how it should be done. Punctuation should fight for its place, just like words.

Stuff you don't need to know

1. The Oxford comma debate/debacle. **If you don't know what the Oxford comma is, you're winning at life.** Don't worry about it. Just focus on keeping your comma use consistent.
2. **Dangling infinitives and split particles** and all that jazz. If it makes sense to you, go for it. I don't care about this stuff if what I write makes sense to me and my reader.

The first step to getting help…

…is admitting you have a problem. My name is Amanda and **I'm addicted to the ellipsis**.

Some people use too many exclamation marks. I've known chronic over-hyphenators. Others love a good dash.

But for me, **it's those three little dots**. They imply an unfinished thought, invite you to draw your own conclusion, or set up a punchline.

A **punctuation tic or quirk** can be part of your personal style. You can pry the ellipsis from my cold, dead hands. (And then bring me a warm cocoa to take off the chill…)

YOUR Super Simple GUIDE TO EDITING and PROOFREADING

In the writing world, there are different types of editing - line editing, copy editing, rewriting, design edits - and they all tend to get lumped together as one thing. For the purposes of this book I'm going to say:

Editing = content + style + grammar

Proofreading = spacing + line breaks + typos + spelling + punctuation + the kitchen sink

Both of these are important, so I'm going to tackle them separately. And I'm going to start with editing.

Editing

Let's get the **APPLES** back in play as a guide for what to pay attention to during this part of the process:

- check your writing focuses on your **AUDIENCE**
- check you've delivered on your **PURPOSE** and focused on one big idea
- check you've done what you said you'd do in your **PLAN**
- check your **LANGUAGE** and tone are working
- **EDIT** and rewrite (here you are)
- check your **STRUCTURE** creates a readable flow, and your formatting makes sense.

Your (basic) editing checklist

- The headline or title is clear and appealing to the reader.
- The **subheadings are consistent** and describe the content.
- The introduction hooks the reader and spells out what's to come.
- There are **no waffle words**, throat clearing or awkward phrases.
- Cut down on using 'that' and 'which'.[12]
- Keep an eye on sentences starting with **'I', 'we', and 'our'**.
- Keep a golden thread running through your work to support your big idea.
- **Watch out for red flag words** such as 'however', 'nonetheless' and 'in reference to' (see The Crap Files on page 83).
- Take back the power and chuck out 'can', 'should', 'will' and 'if'.
- **Take out weak adjectives**, verbs and adverbs.

---

[12] Most writing gets better as soon as you get rid of them. If it forces you to rewrite a sentence? Good.

Two important things to remember:

1. Time *is* on your side

Time is the best editor you'll ever have. When you can let something sit before bringing fresh eyes to the process, **what needs to be cut becomes clear**. (Like making a film, it's what you cut that leaves you with the best result.)

But **editing is also about knowing when to quit** and leave it be.

2. Don't try to edit as you write

It's tempting when you're short on time, but **writing and editing are two different processes**. Keeping them separate makes you a better writer.

> **TIP**
>
> **Use your computer's text-to-speech function** and listen to what you wrote (in a robot voice). If there's a clumsy phrase lurking, this is a great way to weed it out.

Proofreading

Proofreading is the final stage before you print or upload your writing. **It's more straightforward than editing**. But straightforward doesn't mean simple.

Proofreading should pick up spelling, punctuation, syntax and formatting errors. Because it's the **last check for superficial errors**, you've got to catch anything the editing process missed as well as anything that's been amended and doesn't work. And all without messing up the design or layout.

What proofreading isn't

It's not checking the spelling and doing a quick skim. I believe in Spell Check with all my heart, along with the right editing and grammar apps. But nothing can replace a sharp set of eyes reviewing content—especially ones not connected to the hand who wrote it.

Why is proofreading tricky?

You know those jumbled up puzzles where letters are missing but you can still read them? Our natural instinct is to scan and have our brain fill in the gaps. Proofreading is about switching off that natural instinct and **getting clinical about each word**, sentence and paragraph.

If you have to proof your own work, you need **clear boundaries on where proofing begins and ends**. Sneak in an edit here and there if you must, but take the same approach you would if you were proofing someone else's work. Draw a line.

Tread carefully

A proofreader is a little like a doctor—**first, do no harm**. By the time you reach the proofreading stage, the author probably doesn't want any major changes to their content or structure.

Defiant about definite

Do you have a word you never spell right the first time?** Mine is definitely. I want to spell it 'definetely'. And that's not definitely's only problem. There's a tendency for people to trust autocorrect and come up with 'defiantly' instead. I predict in 20 years the words will be interchangeable simply because of how digital use has changed it.* ***Call me on your space phone *and tell me if I was right.*

Your (basic) proofreading checklist

If you can get someone else to proofread your work, think about giving them this list as a way to explain what you do and don't want them to check. Approach it like a conspiracy theory. There are errors to be found. Be suspicious of every punctuation mark.

- Check your document is set to the **right language**. If your setting is UK English and you're writing for a US audience, you're going to miss something.

- Run a **Spell Check**. Note any questionable words you need to double-check, and make sure you've spelled out any abbreviations and acronyms the first time you use them.

- Do a first read through for **obvious style and format issues** like gaps and fonts that don't match.

- **Get more thorough**. Identify words used correctly but inconsistently.

- Check **labelling of figures and graphics** and how they're referred to within the text for consistency.

- Check **headers and footers** are consistent between sections (including page numbers and footnotes).

- Check the **table of contents** matches the actual headings used.

- Check there's enough **white space** between the text. Is the spacing between words, lines, paragraphs and margins correct and consistent? If in doubt, make a note for the designer to check.

- When it comes to professional layout of a document or book, the professional proofreader also looks for **widows** (one word, or the end of a hyphenated word – at the end of a paragraph or column) and **orphans** (a single word, part of a word or very short line that appears at the beginning of a column or a page). Concentrate on it being user-friendly, but don't sweat it too much. Everyone's reading online anyway ;-)

> **TIP**
>
> **Get a professional proofreader** to read through your work and you'll be addicted. They find things you can't, bring a new perspective, and help you sleep at night.

Quick proofreading 'how tos'

If I was one of those writers who called things 'hacks', these would be them. But I'm not.

- Change the font and read it again. It's an easy way to **trick your brain** into seeing something differently.
- Turn your formatting marks on if you're using Word. Don't guess about an extra space between sentences. Fix them now or fix them in the design process (much more expensive).
- In the name of all that is holy, **use Track Changes** or a similar function. It's easier for others to review your work and for you to keep track of what you've done.
- Use a style guide if there is one. But be prepared to break the rules if they don't work for the audience (and you're consistent about it).
- Hold it in your hands. I love printing it out for a **hard copy edit**. There's even a name for that feeling of holding paper in your hand—'the haptic effect'.

Print proof party

In the old days (ahem) when print was more common, **getting the printer's proofs back** after they'd typeset a document was the highlight of my working day. The printer would deliver the proof (and wait if it was urgent), and I'd **mark it up with a red pen** (and pay through the nose for the changes). It was pretty darn exciting to see how the brochure or ad or poster was going to look in print.

These days printer proofs are usually done in PDFs. Or not at all.

TIP

Create a list (get fancy and call it a style sheet) as you proofread a big or complex document. Keep track of any commonly misspelled words, non-negotiable elements (like heading length, tricky acronyms and punctuation quirks), and questions you have about preferred style. Is it cost effective or cost-effective?

Signs and symbols are the oldest forms of communication. (Hieroglyphics much?) Now emoticons have evolved into emojis, a **living and breathing language** all of their own.

Whether you ♥ or 👎 emojis, they're a part of our word world and may be the truly universal language. Sure, everyone brings their own interpretation to symbols. But they do the same with words.

Emojis **bring emotion to content** that doesn't always exist in words alone. When it comes to words on a page, italics and a handful of punctuation marks are all we have to add nuance and emotion without spelling it out.

Think of what an 😕 can convey in one symbol. Not to mention the cultural meanings some emojis are assigned. (Ahem... eggplant.) They are part of a rich and evolving language.

Using **emojis in your writing can work**, but beware the thin line between 'a shortcut to understanding' and 'trying too hard'.

Emoji action

Can emojis be used as part of my writing? 👍 👍

Should I use emoji on my loan application or in a report to a Board?

Could I use emojis on an application to be social media manager for a funky brand? 🤘 👏

Could I use emojis in work emails to a desk buddy I know well?

Could I use emojis in work emails to my boss or someone I don't know well? 🤔 👎

What are the top five emojis to avoid in all but totally personal texts?

Are emojis a valid form of communication when used well?

Emojis work when ...

They're **simple and complement language** instead of replacing it.

You can order a Domino's pizza by tweeting them .

Emojis don't work when ...

They get **too complicated. Or kind of sexist**, like the below that appeared in an ad. So the high-heel emoji is telling us the female spends too much on shoes? But a burger makes a man happy again? Ugh.

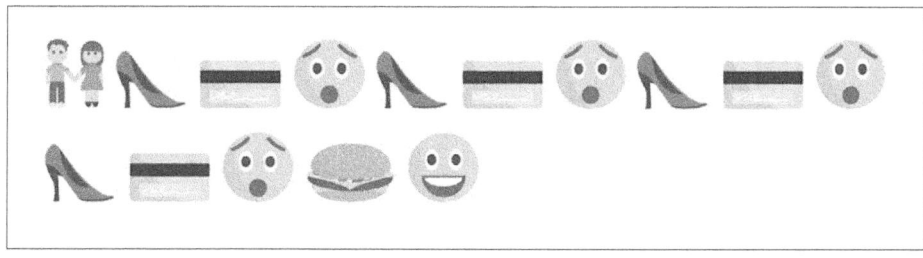

Before I head into the next section of this book which is about writing better emails, blog posts and ransom notes, I need to take a quick time out and introduce you to THE CRAP FILES. Words that should be burnt at the stake.

But first ...

Pssst, secret squirrel

When it comes to writing there's no such thing as 'never' or 'always'.

So, I'll admit I use these words sometimes. And if they make sense to your audience, you can too.

But most of the time, eliminating the following words from your writing will make it stronger and better. Use them with care:

herewith – "Hey, 1903 called. They want their word back."

aforementioned – See above.

irregardless – Debate rages (well, for me) over whether this is the world's most superfluous word. Is it even a word? I demand it's expulsion from the dictionary Pluto style.

moreover – Huh?

the period of time – time

in relation to – about

I would like to take this opportunity to… – Be like Nike. Just say it.

that – Most sentences will still make sense without it. Delete it and your writing will be better.

really – Think really, really hard about whether you need it.

very – A lazy way to emphasise something. Be specific.

just – A filler word. Delete it and see if it ruins your sentence.

our aim is to… – Don't be weak. Say definitively what you do or deliver. No need to ask for permission.

furthermore – Just start your sentence already!

encompassed within – part of

as an organisation – pointless

very unique – Oh Lord, help us.

write BETTER EMAILS

They really should give awards for well-written emails. They can get you a raise, build businesses, and make you look super smart.

We write emails to friends, companies and customers every day. It's such an everyday thing, **it's easy to forget how important they are**. And sometimes it's hard to get a straight answer... or even a reply.

Writing better emails sets you up as a go-to contact who knows their stuff. Here's how...

Make the subject line matter

- **Never leave it blank.** Ever. The element of surprise is not your friend.
- **Think like a newspaper headline.** A teaser keeps them reading.
- **Be specific.** Make your email easier to find later. Call something "Apple Pie Slicer Project meeting – August 2022" not "Steering group from last week".

> **TIP**
>
> **Break the chain. Remove FW:** from forwarded emails and rename them. Emails starting with FW: FW: FW: FW: FW: meeting go to the bottom of my to-do list.

Keep it simple and relevant

- **Get to the point.** Don't overload your audience with more than they asked for.
- **Avoid long chunks of text.** You'll lose the reader if they have to work too hard. Dot points are your friend.
- **Write to be forwarded on.** Don't be paranoid, but writing as if anyone could read your email keeps you focussed, professional and 'on message'.

Give them something to do

- **Be clear about what they need to do next.** Spell out if you want them to respond, give feedback, accept an invitation or whatever.
- **Make it easy to respond.** Give clear deadlines and contact details.
- **Don't bury what you need in a long email.** Ask for what you need, discuss it briefly, and then ask again.

Stand up and be counted

- **Don't kick off with an apology.** Starting on a negative note lowers the confidence of your tone and your credibility.
- **Be direct.** You can say what you mean and still be likeable.
- **Show your smarts.** Don't downplay your understanding or ask for permission to disagree.

Cracking the work email code

Your name without a "Hi" in front – *Brace yourself. You're in trouble.*

"Have a great day" – *Have a terrible day filled with bad things.*

"As per my email on Tuesday at 2.37pm…" – *Stop ignoring my emails, you animal. And now I've had to CC the boss.*

"Just a quick reminder…" – *This won't be quick, and you're on thin ice.*

"We need to try harder" – *You need to try harder.*

SHOW ME

Even the basics of life are easier when you write better emails. For example, let's say you see a sofa bed in a store on Saturday. Gary the sales assistant gives you a discount code you can use online. But when you're ready to order you can't find the code.

 Subject: online

I had a discount code and now I can't find it. I want to buy something now. Can I still get a discount?

 Subject: Sofa bed discount code

Hi Gary

Could you please let me know the online discount code for the sofa bed we discussed on Saturday? It was model T3001 – the Braydon 2-seater in brown suede.

Thanks,
Sofia

> **TIP**
>
> **Writing a great email is like making a great sandwich.** Tell them the important thing or big idea (the first slice of bread), add some information (butter and their favourite filling), and then tell them the important thing again (the other slice of bread). Hungry?

If you only remember one thing: **get to the point.**

write BETTER JOB STUFF

The better writer always gets the job.

Don't let Jan get that promotion over you. You deserve it. Beat her at her own game with a clear job application that gets you hired.

The traditional job application process is painful for nearly everyone involved. The person hiring usually starts by sorting them into three piles—"Yes", "No" and "Maybe". Quick decisions are made by glancing at the CV to see whether the person has qualifications, vaguely relevant experience, and can spell their own name.

Be the better writer and give your career a massive boost.

It's a jungle out there

I've seen job applications that would curl your hair. CVs a paragraph long and 13 pages long. Cover letters in an 8-point font with 2mm margins. **Glamour photos of the applicant.** Addressing selection criteria for a completely different job, with placeholder headlines and text such as 'add better example here'. Such is the rich tapestry of humanity.

Do as you're told

- **Follow the formatting instructions.** They want Arial 11pt double spaced with 2.5cm margins? Sure thing.
- **Read between the lines.** Forget tangents or cramming in big words. Take a breath and look at what the question is really asking.

Less is more

- **Remember your goal.** You want an interview. So give them enough information to make you an obvious choice, not your life story.
- **Know when to let go.** Stop listing that paper route you gave up on your 10th birthday.

Keep it professional

- **Go easy on the details of your social life.** They'll stalk you on social media anyway. Put your efforts into checking your privacy settings.
- **Don't get cocky.** You might be perfect, but don't use vaguely threatening phrases such as, "You'd be lucky to have me".

Dot your i's and cross your t's

- **Pay attention.** Typo? Bye. Unreadable font? Bye. Forgot to change the company name from your last application? Bye.
- **Formatting counts.** Use dot points, tables, bolding and whatever else helps make it scannable.

TIPS

We know your name. Please don't introduce yourself in the first line of your cover letter. ("Hi, my name is Amanda.") Just don't.

Speak their language. Try to mirror the language of the application in your response. But don't use a word you wouldn't say out loud in an interview.

Be a STAR

An oldie but a goldie, the STAR method takes the pain out of answering selection criteria questions. Talking through a structured example helps the person assessing your application tick a box on their list.

Highlight the non-negotiable skills, something refreshing to set you apart, and practical examples that make it easy for them to see you have experience.

SITUATION – what was going on, where you were working and the circumstances to set the scene for your example.

TASK – what needed to be achieved and why (measurable targets are always a bonus – if you achieved them).

ACTION – what you did, why you did it, and how you did it.

RESPONSE – what happened next. Did you reach the target? Solve a problem? Get positive feedback? Give us a happy ending.

A lot of job descriptions have the same stilted, formal and unrealistic language. **Cut through the crap** and think about what they really want to know.

SHOW ME

You're applying for a job at The Rock Farm, an organic farm and restaurant. You're asked to provide an example of how you've coped with a challenge in the workplace. (Yes, it's vague. Just like in real life.)

I enjoy coping with a challenge in the workplace. (You also seem to enjoy meaningless repetition.)

When I was working at SupaFarm I faced many challenging situations that enabled me to step up and support the team to get the job done. I am confident in my demonstrated ability to manage challenges at Rock Farm. (You're not applying for a job at the cliché factory. I have no idea what you did at SupaFarm.)

S As Produce Manager at SupaFarm, I was responsible for delivering fresh produce orders daily to on-site restaurant kitchens.

T The event and kitchen teams were frustrated by issues with not enough or too much produce being supplied.

SHOW ME

A To improve communication, I trialled morning catch-up meetings with representatives from each team.

R The meetings developed new relationships and encouraged collaboration across teams. I was proud to receive a Staff Recognition award for my role in solving this challenge.

TIP

Go with the flow. Use the STAR headings when you draft your application, and delete them before you send it. It should flow without headings as a clear example of a problem you solved.

write BETTER RaNSOM NoTeS

If the day comes when you ~~finally snap~~ have to write a ransom note, you need to convey your demands quickly and clearly.

It's not just important to get the message across—someone's life (or bear with an unnerving sentimental attachment) could depend on it.

True (crime) love

I inherited a love of crime and procedural forensic dramas from my mum and my grandma. If Law and Order and Ian Rankin have taught me anything, it's that **the ransom note is usually the ultimate undoing of the perp**. *Write better and change the narrative.*

Top tips for untrackable ransom notes

Get straight to the point

This has never been more important. Establish:

- what has happened so far
- what you want
- what happens next.

Be specific

Don't say, "Drop the bag of cash in the park on Smyth Street". Go for, "Drop the bag in the third green rubbish bin to the left of the apple tree on the south side of the Smyth Street park at 3.15pm".

Tone down the backstory

Elaborate backstories are your enemy in the ransom note game. At this moment it's not about the why or the could-have-beens. This is a transaction. Don't overthink it or try to be clever: you'll leave too many clues.

SHOW ME

You've captured your spouse's teddy bear and want to exchange it for loading the dishwasher. Go.

I'm so sick of always being the one to load the dishwasher. Why don't you ever do it without being asked? It's so infuriating. I've taken Baron Von Bearington. He's safe for now, but I won't release him until the dishwasher is packed. I'm sorry it has come to this.

Pack it properly, and clean up any other dishes lying around. And hand wash the crusty saucepan you've avoided for three weeks. That's so typical of you. You've driven me to this.

When you've packed the dishwasher, I'll let the Beebs go.

And don't call the police or tell anyone.

This is a confession, not a ransom note. Take the emotion out and stick to what's happening, action required and specific details. Resist using the Baron's pet name. It indicates emotional attachment that makes it unlikely you'll follow through on your threat.

SHOW ME

👍 **We have Baron Von Bearington.**

Don't call the police. Or your mum.

To ensure his safe return, **pack the dishwasher. And hand wash the crusty saucepan.**

Send a Snap of the packed dishwasher to didn't_do_it_84 and you'll receive **instructions** on the return of your bear.

Much better. 'We' throws them off the scent. You've identified early what they might do instinctively, and given them clear instruction not to (and the consequences). You've provided specifics on what to do next.

Now, we wait...

Bad PowerPoint can happen to good people.

For God's sake Trevor, read one more of those slides word-for-word. Just one more and I'm going out the window. Doesn't open? I'll quietly excuse myself and hide in the toilet for 15 minutes. I'd rather be suspected of explosive diarrhoea than hear one more slide being read out.

Poor old PowerPoint gets a bad rap. But **don't blame the software**. It was designed to present data and graphs. The rest of us hijacked it to torture workmates, bosses and people we're training.

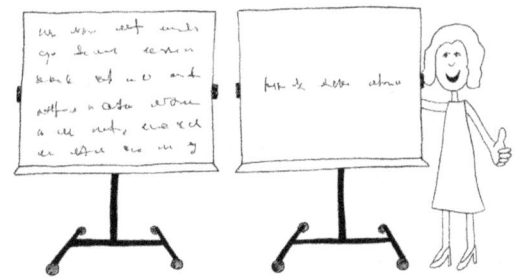

Seeing it as **more than a tool to keep eyes on the screen and off you** is the first step to standing out with better presentations.

Fight the fear

"If I don't have everything on the slides they'll think I'm leaving stuff out, or that I don't know all the background."

No, they won't. That's what the **Notes function** is for. Some of the most memorable presentations I've seen had one slide or none at all. And I never felt they didn't know their stuff.

Forget what anyone thinks of your format or how many slides you do or don't use. Concentrate on **what you want them to remember** about your topic.

Audience first

It's always about the audience. Even if you're presenting about yourself, it's about the audience. No exceptions. Every part of your presentation is influenced by what they need.

People remember what you say at the start and the end. For the rest **they'll just remember how they felt**—interested, bored, inspired, pained. You decide.

Structure

Have so little actual text on the slides that **no-one asks for a copy of the presentation**. They won't need to, because they've already taken in what you want them to know.

Language

Read the room. If you're delivering a casual presentation to workmates you can use more relaxed language.

If you're doing a formal presentation to a board or an investor, be explanatory without being patronising. **Jargon is fine** if that's where your audience is comfortable.

Editing and drafts

Try a new approach. Instead of cutting and pasting content directly from a report into slides, paste it into the Notes section. **Then make each word fight to make it above the line.**

Presentations without too much content mean people *listen* instead of *reading* word-for-word what the presenter says.

Content

Don't worry if you don't present exactly how you planned. **The audience can't see the Notes section**, and so they have no idea what you were planning.

> **TIP**
>
> **Don't start by thanking the audience.** Start with a strong statement you want them to remember. Your big idea. Then thank them.

SHOW ME

Don't obsess over slides. How many slides you have has no correlation with your presentation skills or your value as a human. Which of these slides would get your attention?

- You should never write too much on a slide and then read it out to your audience
- Too much information will make your audience tune out and forget the important parts of what you have to say
- Most of us have almost fallen asleep in a presentation or started to write our shopping list
- Learn to do better presentations

Is anyone writing their shopping list?

TIP

Question everything. If you have to choose between wrapping up early and leaving time for questions, or running over, cut yourself off. Every time.

write BETTER apologies

If you're in the wrong, apologise early and often. Whoever you're saying sorry to may not be in the right, but a good apology doesn't care.

If you're apologising in work or your business, customers can have a real effect on your reputation in a very short time. Customers have high expectations. And social media means they're no longer a faceless mass. If something has gone wrong **take a breath, leave your ego at the door, and think** about how everyone can get what they want.

And if you need to say sorry to someone you care about, it's even more important to get it right.

Say it like you mean it

Say sorry. Don't muddy the waters with "I regret", "I withdraw my comment", or other crap. Even worse, don't deflect the apology with a reference to being sorry someone was offended, or that they took something out of context or without a sense of humour.

Do

- Be clear on the problem, why you're apologising, and who you're apologising to
- Apologise early and often
- If you're apologising on social media, keep it short, sweet and consistent. Communicate like the world is watching
- Try to be relatable and likeable. Putting a human face to a mistake makes it easier to forgive

Don't

- Be defensive or shift blame
- Ridicule, belittle or criticise anyone you need to apologise to
- Engage with trolls (unless your business makes troll bridges and they're your key target market)
- Make promises you can't or won't keep
- Use big words or jargon to intimidate, confuse or control

SHOW ME

When it's done well:

When KFC in the UK had "teething problems" with a new supplier, stores across the country ran out of chicken. (Kind of an important element of their brand.)

The chain apologised to customers through a series of print and social media ads featuring the famous chicken bucket with KFC replaced with 'FCK'.

They thanked customers for sticking with a "chicken restaurant without any chicken" and used #WheresMyChicken across Twitter so users could find their nearest open KFC store.

Well played.

SHOW ME

When it's not done well:

Organisers were forced to apologise about the service and facilities at a pricey Sydney Harbour New Year's Eve event. Here are some of the lowlights.

"the event, which required significant financial investment and took over six months in planning" (We don't care)

"all parties involved have been working diligently to formulate a response" (Still don't care)

"our commitment to delivering a variety of fairly complex dishes was too high" (Oh, so you tried too hard)

"A formal process is in place to address the current climate surrounding the event" (Huh?)

We're sorry for the service and facilities issues at the event.

Thank you for your patience. We're working through your feedback, and will make another statement on Tuesday about next steps.

That wasn't so hard. Say sorry and give a specific timeframe for your next move.

write BETTER HEADLINES AND HEADINGS

You have milliseconds to stand out online. To catch your audience's eye, hook them and keep them, your headlines and headings need to promise something meaningful.

Make the grade with A+ headings

- Promise to solve a problem or answer a question.
- Be specific. *37 ways to clean a homing pigeon* is a **specific headline solving a problem** for a specific audience.
- Be consistent. Set a word or character limit for headlines in a single document or within your blog. **Help your reader** settle into the style and stay engaged.

Your clickable glossary

Click bait: *appeals to your curiosity or voyeuristic tendencies with a headline that sucks you in (sometimes against your better judgement).*

Click worthy: *makes a clickable promise and then delivers with credible content.*

Click candy: *a guilty pleasure that's the kinder, gentler cousin of click bait. It's okay to sweeten the deal to grab someone's attention if you deliver what you've promised.*

Click and stick: *starts as click worthy and is so good your reader stays and then goes down a rabbit hole of your content (boosted by smart crosslinking of your articles).*

Click pic: *an image powerful enough to get clicks with little text or a headline that implies you'll learn more.*

Click wrist: *see scroll wrist, scroll finger and thumb ache.*

Pre-click evacuation: *clicking on an article, immediately regretting it and quickly clicking back or onto something else before the page loads.*

write BETTER BLOGS

Blogs aren't just about cats, coffee or introspective angst anymore. They're creative outlets, community builders, and often a first step for businesses (large and small) into the heady world of content marketing.

But... the information superhighway is gridlocked by bloggers, vloggers and phloggers. So forget Field of Dreams—*if you build your blog, they won't necessarily come and read it. Writing well makes a huge difference here.*

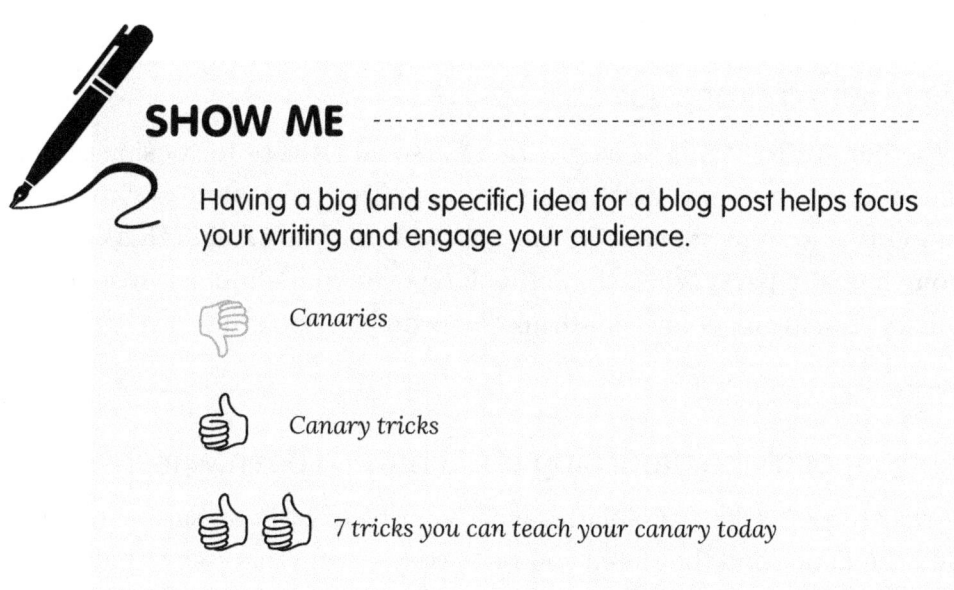

SHOW ME

Having a big (and specific) idea for a blog post helps focus your writing and engage your audience.

👎 *Canaries*

👍 *Canary tricks*

👍👍 *7 tricks you can teach your canary today*

What better bloggers do

Make their readers' lives easier with 'aha' moments

Every blog is ultimately about making something easier for your audience. If they're a crochet nut, 7 *steps to choosing the perfect wool* makes their life easier.

Write with a strong voice

Whether you're writing a blog with a personal slant or for business, find a consistent tone of voice. It's okay to write the way you talk (with fewer ummms) and show some personality. How would you **explain this topic to someone at a party** when they're looking over your shoulder, wondering if they should go get another drink? How do you hook them in?

Write like that.

Know that all the great blog posts haven't been written

Ideas are everywhere, no matter what your topic is. Look hard enough at your audience and they'll tell you what they want. What's new that needs explaining? **What do people want help with?** What's an experience they'd relate to? If you're not sure, ask them.

How to get the thing written

1. Start with a specific working title to keep you on track.
2. Get a structure going by adding subheadings for sections you want to cover.
3. Add dot points under each heading to create an outline and see how it flows.
4. Be clear in your introduction what the blog post's purpose is, and why your audience should keep reading.
5. Write. Get the page dirty.
6. Keep. Going.
7. If you have data or evidence to back up your claims, use it in a smart and simple way.
8. Leave it alone.
9. Edit.
10. Leave it alone.
11. Rewrite if needed.
12. Leave it alone.
13. Proofread.
14. Publish.
15. Go back to step 1.

> **TIP**
>
> **Know the difference between evergreen or topical content.** Evergreen content doesn't date, while topical content hangs on a trend, something in the news or an event happening now.

If you only remember one thing: **blog to solve a problem or answer a specific question.**

You're no doubt one of the three-point-something billion people[13] *around the globe using social media. Throw apps into the mix and there are* **thousands of social (and quite anti-social)** *platforms at your disposal. If you're like me you both love it and hate it (depending on the time of day).*

Social media is more than the audience asking, "So what?" They scan quicker, judge harsher, and instantly want to know, "What's in it for me?"

Don't assume you can phone it in when you're writing social media content. Quite the opposite. **Your writing chops really matter here.** Writing well on socials can put a spotlight on your personal profile or brand. And **a misstep can ping around the world in 80 seconds.**

The long and the short of social media

Know where your audience hangs out online and write in a way that suits those platforms. LinkedIn is generally more formal and professional, while Twitter is snarky and irreverent. But remember, rules and conventions shift all the time.

---

[13] *Digital in 2018 Global Overview*

Think about how your reader will see what you write (most likely on their phone), and how it'll work as a piece they'll need to scroll through. Will your heading make sense if it's cut off? Will the image engage them without the caption?

Treat a social post like any other piece of writing. Know who it's for, use the right language, edit, rewrite and proofread. Yes, most people scan your content, but always write for the person who reads every word. The best writing always looks like it took no time at all. Be like the swimming duck—gliding effortlessly on the surface, with its little legs underneath kicking like crazy.

Avoid showing the sausage

If you're working across a range of social media platforms, try to change up your content for each one. Posting the same content on every platform might hit the right note for one of them, but not all of them. And even if you change your tone, anyone who follows you across all your platforms will see the lazy way a social media sausage is made.

Which platform should you back?

Whichever one your audience is backing. (Are you using the same social platforms you did five years ago? Probably not.) **Stick to producing smart content and being ready to adapt to changing formats.** *Follow the trends for content being consumed on mobiles, video and voice controls –* **trends cut across platforms***. Whatever the next big thing is in social, good writing that focuses on your audience will always be part of its success.*

SHOW ME

Let's take a look at a social post for a small business accountant. Our purpose is building awareness and leading the audience to the website… and our big idea is linked to helping time-poor small business owners enjoy life (and business) again.

STARTING OUT

 Our job at Aardvark Accountants is to help you with your business books and accounts so you can save time. We can prepare your tax returns and balance your books.

(Clumsy wording, with a focus on 'our' and 'we'.)

SHARPENING FOR SOCIAL

 Want to put the kids to bed?

Choosing the right accountant gets you home earlier and means everyone gets a better night's sleep.

Read 7 questions to ask your small business accountant and find out if you're in the best hands.

(This version creates an emotional connection, links it to a choice they can make, and gives them somewhere to go next. And remember, the image you choose can make or break whether the post cuts through. Showing a satisfied mum or dad looking over sleeping kids means more to your business owner than a picture of coins and cash.)

If you only remember one thing: **you won't get away with crap writing on socials.**

If you're short on time, here's the shortcut guaranteed to make you a better writer.

READ.

Feed your brain and read everything you can.

READ.

I read my junk mail. I read the free supermarket magazines full of recipes I'll never make. I read the back of the cereal box as I eat my breakfast. I read small print, big headings and signs wherever I go. I'm addicted.

Offer to read the work of others and learn from it. Sharpening your editing and proofreading skills on others makes your writing better.

Pay attention

Don't underestimate the power of thinking time. If you're writing Facebook ads, **pay attention to what cuts through** and read as many as you can. If you're writing a blog, think about the topic and possible angles and headlines while you wait for the kettle to boil. Switch on your writing brain and be inspired by the world around you.

Fall in love with words

There's a saying that feeling good makes you shine like a sunbeam. Or something like that. Well, wanting to write well shines through too. We don't always have the luxury of writing things that light us up. But **if you commit to writing better and falling in love with words, it shows** no matter what you're writing.

What next?

I'd love to hear from you! Tell me what you think about the book (and what you want to see in the next one).

Visit: www.writebetter.com.au

Email: hello@writebetter.com.au

Facebook: www.facebook.com/writebetterbook

Twitter: @avanelderen

Instagram: @amandavanelderen

Acknowledgements

My **family**, who I love more than their tiny brains can comprehend.

My **mum and my Mama** who gave me a love of words. (Sorry my first book couldn't have been a police procedural set in Scotland. Next time.)

The **friends** who love me without a legal obligation. Suckers.

Kelly for her book coaching, the structural editing I didn't know I needed, design and general awesomeness. **Amy**, the artist and illustrator who reads my mind to make crazy ideas come to life. **Bill** for sharpening it all up. Let's do it again soon. (NB: Anything awesome, they helped me do it. Any mistakes are my own.)

#NCR shout out to the **copy beasts**. Thanks for being there and to KT for so very much.

The **Write Better Facebook group**. (Come join us!)

Everyone who responded to the **pre-book survey**. You made this book better.

To everyone who had enough faith to **preorder the book** (and not hold your breath while I got it done).

www.ingramcontent.com/pod-product-compliance
Lightning Source LLC
Chambersburg PA
CBHW080347300426
44110CB00019B/2529